**LEADERSHIP BEYOND AUTHORITY**
"The Secret Of Sustainable Leadership Success"

BY

A.O Osborne

Copyright Page

© 2024 [A.O Osborne] All rights reserved.

No part of this publication may be reproduced, distributed, or transmitted in any form or by any means, including photocopying, recording, or other electronic or mechanical methods, without the prior written permission of the publisher, except in the case of brief quotations embodied in critical reviews and certain other noncommercial uses permitted by copyright law. For permissions, contact the author and publisher

A. O Osborne.

**Dedication**

To the entire members of the Global Network of Impact Leaders(GNIL), whose commitment to creating positive change in the world continues to inspire and motivate me. Your dedication to excellence and leadership is a beacon of hope and transformation.

And to my beloved children, Manasseh, Favour, Sharon, and Michelle. Your love and joy are the greatest gifts of my life. This book is a testament to the dreams I hold for your future and the legacy I hope to leave for you.

With all my love,

A.O Osborne.

## Acknowledgment

Writing "Leadership Beyond Authority: The Secret of Sustainable Leadership Success" has been a journey of deep reflection and immense growth. I owe a debt of gratitude to many individuals who have played a pivotal role in this process.

First and foremost, I would like to express my heartfelt gratitude to my spiritual father and mentor, Charles Osazuwa. Your wisdom, guidance, and unwavering support have been instrumental in shaping my understanding of leadership and success. Your teachings have provided a strong foundation upon which this book is built.

To my beloved wife, Gift, your love, patience, and encouragement have been my anchor throughout this journey. Your belief in me has been a source of strength and inspiration. I am eternally grateful for your unwavering support.

To my dear friend, Sam. E whose insights and feedback have enriched this work, thank you for your invaluable contributions. Your perspective has been a constant reminder of the importance of friendship and collaboration.

Lastly, to my family, your constant love and support have been a cornerstone in my life. You have always been there for me, and for that, I am profoundly grateful.

Thank you all for being a part of this journey. This book is a testament to your impact on my life and my leadership journey.

With gratitude,

A. O Osborne.

# ABOUT THE AUTHOR

 A. O. Osborne is a multifaceted author and expert whose works span across several influential niches. With a deep-seated passion for enriching lives, Osborne writes on food and diet, relationship and sex, personal development, health and fitness, cooking, financial markets and leadership. His extensive knowledge and practical insights offer readers valuable guidance and inspiration in these diverse areas.

As a professional forex trader, Osborne brings a unique perspective to his writing. He not only excels in the financial markets but also dedicates himself to mentoring others in the intricacies of forex trading. His ability to simplify complex concepts and his commitment to his students' success have earned him a reputation as a respected mentor in the trading community.

Osborne's personal life is a testament to his values and dedication. He is married to Gift, and together they are raising four lovely children. His family life enriches his understanding of relationships, further informing his work and adding depth to his writing on personal development and family dynamics.

Through his books, A. O. Osborne aims to empower individuals to lead healthier, more fulfilling lives, achieve personal and professional growth, and navigate the complexities of modern relationships and financial independence. His writing is not just informative but transformative, offering practical advice that readers can apply to their everyday lives.

Table of Contents

**Introduction**
**Redefining Leadership**

The necessity of evolving leadership paradigms
Brief overview of traditional vs. modern leadership
The concept of sustainable leadership: definitions and importance
Author's journey and reasons for writing this book
Overview of the book's structure and key takeaways

Chapter 1
**The Essence of Sustainable Leadership**

Detailed definition of sustainable leadership
Characteristics of sustainable leaders:
Visionary thinking
Ethical grounding
Long-term orientation
Commitment to personal and team growth
Benefits of sustainable leadership:
Enhanced team performance
Long-term organizational success
Positive social and environmental impact
Examples of sustainable leadership in action:
Case studies of renowned leaders and organizations
Comparative analysis of traditional vs. sustainable leadership outcomes

Chapter 2
**Cultivating a Leadership Mindset**

The growth mindset:
Carol Dweck's research and its implications for leaders
Practical steps to develop a growth mindset
Self-awareness and reflection:

Importance of knowing your strengths and weaknesses
Tools for self-assessment (e.g., SWOT analysis, 360-degree feedback)
Emotional intelligence:
Components of emotional intelligence (self-awareness, self-regulation, motivation, empathy, social skills)
Techniques for enhancing emotional intelligence
Practical exercises:
Journaling for self-reflection
Role-playing scenarios to build emotional intelligence

## Chapter 3
### Vision Beyond Authority

Crafting a compelling vision:
Elements of a strong vision statement
Aligning vision with organizational values and mission
Communicating your vision:
Techniques for effective communication
Engaging storytelling and its impact
Inspiring and mobilizing others:
Methods to motivate and engage your team
Building consensus and buy-in
Real-world examples:
Leaders who transformed their organizations through visionary leadership

## Chapter 4
### Building Trust and Credibility

Foundations of trust in leadership:
Transparency, consistency, and reliability
Earning and maintaining credibility:
The role of expertise and competence
Demonstrating integrity and ethical behavior
Strategies for building trust:
Open communication
Honoring commitments

Recognizing and rectifying mistakes
Case studies:
Examples of leaders who successfully built trust and credibility
Analysis of failures and lessons learned

## Chapter 5
**Empoweringand Enabling Others**

The importance of delegation:
Benefits of effective delegation
Overcoming barriers to delegation
Coaching and mentoring:
Distinctions between coaching and mentoring
Techniques for effective coaching and mentoring
Creating a supportive environment
Fostering psychological safety
Encouraging creativity and innovation
Real-world applications:
Success stories of empowered teams
Practical tips for leaders to empower their teams

## Chapter 6
**Leading ThroughInfluence,Not Authority**

The power of influence:
Understanding influence and its impact
Difference between influence and authority
Techniques for leading through influence:
Building relationships and networks
Persuasion and negotiation skills
Case studies:
Leaders who excelled without formal authority
Analysis of their methods and strategies
Practical exercises:
Developing your influence skills through practice and feedback

## Chapter 7

### Navigating Ethical Dilemmas

The importance of ethics in leadership:
Defining ethical leadership
Long-term benefits of ethical behavior
Frameworks for ethical decision-making:
Utilitarianism, deontology, and virtue ethics
Practical decision-making models (e.g., Kidder's Ethical Decision-Making Model)
Real-world examples:
Leaders facing ethical dilemmas and their resolutions
Lessons learned from both successes and failures
Practical tips:
How to develop an ethical culture within your organization
Encouraging ethical behavior among team members

### Chapter 8
**Fostering Innovationand Adaptability....47**

Encouraging a culture of innovation:
Creating an environment conducive to creativity
Recognizing and rewarding innovative ideas
Leading through change and uncertainty:
Strategies for managing change
Communicating change effectively
Maintaining adaptability:
Importance of flexibility in leadership
Tools and techniques for staying adaptable
Case studies:
Organizations that thrived through innovation and adaptability
Leadership practices that supported their success

### Chapter 9
**Building and Sustaining Resilient Teams**

Characteristics of resilient teams:

Cohesion, trust, and adaptability
Strategies for team building:
Techniques for fostering team spirit and unity
Activities and exercises to build resilience
Handling team conflicts:
Conflict resolution strategies
Turning conflicts into opportunities for growth
Real-world examples:
Case studies of resilient teams and their achievements
Analysis of leadership practices that fostered resilience

## Chapter 10
**Achieving Sustainable, Long-term Success**

Defining sustainable success:
Key performance indicators for sustainable leadership
Tools and metrics for measurement:
Balanced Scorecard, OKRs (Objectives and Key Results)
Feedback mechanisms and continuous improvement
Continuous learning and development:
Importance of lifelong learning
Resources for ongoing leadership development
Real-world applications:
Case studies of leaders and organizations that achieved sustainable success
Lessons and best practices

**Conclusion**: The Journey of Sustainable Leadership
Recap of key principles and takeaways
Encouragement for continuous growth and development
Call to action: inspiring readers to implement sustainable leadership practices
Final thoughts and reflections on the future of leadership

# INTRODUCTION

Preface reconsidering Leadership In the dynamic and fleetly evolving world we live in moment, the traditional conception of leadership is being challenged and reshaped. The hierarchical, authority- driven model of leadership that formerly dominated commercial and organizational geographies is no longer sufficient. The complications of ultramodern business, coupled with the adding interconnectivity of global requests and societies, demand a new kind of leadership — bone that's sustainable, inclusive, and adaptive. This book,"Leadership Beyond Authority The Secret of Sustainable Leadership Success," explores this new paradigm of leadership. It delves into what it means to lead effectively in a period where power and influence are earned through trust, vision, and ethical geste
, rather than through positional authority alone. The Evolving Landscape of Leadership Historically, leadership was frequently equated with authority. The leader was the person in charge, the bone who made the opinions and applied control. still, as the world has come more complex and connected, this model has shown its limitations. moment, effective leadership is lower about issuing commands and further about inspiring and guiding others toward a participated vision. It's about creating an terrain where people can thrive, introduce, and contribute to a lesser good. Why Traditional Authority Is No Longer Enough In the history, leaders could calculate on their positional power to drive performance. But in the ultramodern plant, this approach is decreasingly ineffective. workers moment seek meaning and purpose in their work; they want to be part of commodity bigger than themselves. They're more engaged and productive when they feel valued, heard, and empowered. thus, sustainable leadership is about impacting and inspiring people rather than simply directing them. The Concept of Sustainable Leadership Sustainable leadership is embedded in principles that insure long- term success and positive impact. It's about leading in a way that benefits not only the association but also its people, its community, and the terrain. Sustainable leaders are visionary, ethical, and flexible. They concentrate on erecting trust, fostering invention, and nurturing gift. They

understand that true leadership extends beyond the confines of their authority and seeks to produce continuing value. My trip and Why I Wrote This Book. My trip into understanding and championing for sustainable leadership began with my own gests in colorful leadership places. I witnessed firsthand the limitations of traditional, authority-grounded leadership and the profound impact of a further inclusive, empowering approach. This book is the capstone of times of literacy, observing, and rehearsing these principles. It's my attempt to partake these perceptivity and to help aspiring leaders navigate the complications of ultramodern leadership. What You Can Anticipate from This Book " Beyond Authority- The Secret of Sustainable Leadership Success" is structured to give you with both the theoretical underpinnings and practical operations of sustainable leadership. Each chapter delves into crucial aspects of leadership, offering practicable strategies, real- world exemplifications, and reflective exercises to help you develop and upgrade your leadership chops. You'll learn about - The essential traits and benefits of sustainable leadership - Cultivating a growth mindset and emotional intelligence - Crafting and communicating a compelling vision - structure trust and credibility within your platoon - Empowering others and leading through influence - Navigating ethical dilemmas and fostering invention - structure flexible brigades and measuring sustainable success. A Roadmap for Aspiring Leaders- This book is designed to be a roadmap for anyone aspiring to lead in a way that's poignant, ethical, and enduring. Whether you're a seasoned superintendent, amid-level director, or an arising leader, the principles and practices outlined in this book will give you with the tools you need to lead effectively in moment's complex world. The Journey Begins As you embark on this trip of sustainable leadership, flash back that leadership isn't a destination but a nonstop process of growth and literacy. The principles and strategies in this book are meant to guide and inspire you, but the true metamorphosis comes from your commitment to applying them in your diurnal life and work. I invite you to join me in exploring the secrets of sustainable leadership success. Let's move beyond authority and discover the profound impact of leading with vision, integrity, and a genuine desire to make a difference. Welcome to

Leadership Beyond Authority "The Secret of Sustainable Leadership Success."

Chapter 1

## The Essence of Sustainable Leadership-Introduction to Sustainable Leadership

Sustainable leadership transcends the traditional boundaries of authority and focuses on fostering long-term success and positive impact. It emphasizes the importance of ethical behavior, visionary thinking, and a commitment to continuous improvement. Sustainable leaders inspire trust, cultivate innovation, and create environments where people can thrive. This chapter explores the foundational principles of sustainable leadership and the characteristics that define effective sustainable leaders.

### Defining Sustainable Leadership

Sustainable leadership is an approach that prioritizes long-term organizational health, environmental stewardship, and social responsibility. Unlike traditional leadership, which often focuses on short-term gains and immediate results, sustainable leadership is concerned with enduring success and the well-being of all stakeholders. This holistic approach considers the interconnectedness of business, society, and the environment.

### Key Traits of Sustainable Leaders

Effective sustainable leaders exhibit several key traits that set them apart from traditional leaders:

1. **Visionary** Thinking:Sustainable leaders have a clear and compelling vision for the future. They can see beyond the immediate challenges and opportunities to understand the long-term implications of their actions. This vision guides their decision-making and inspires others to work towards a shared goal.

2. **Ethical Grounding:** Integrity and ethical behavior are at the core of sustainable leadership. These leaders prioritize honesty, transparency, and fairness in all their interactions. They make decisions based on a strong moral compass, ensuring that their actions align with their values and the greater good.

3. **Long-Term Orientation**: Sustainable leaders focus on creating lasting value. They understand that short-term gains should not come at the expense of long-term sustainability. This perspective influences their strategic planning, resource allocation, and stakeholder engagement.

4. **Commitment to Personal and TeamGrowth**: Continuous learning and development are crucial for sustainable leaders. They invest in their growth and the growth of their team members. By fostering a culture of learning, they ensure that their organization remains adaptable and innovative.

### Benefits of Sustainable Leadership

Sustainable leadership offers numerous benefits for organizations and society as a whole:

1. **Enhanced Team Performance**: By creating a positive and supportive work environment, sustainable leaders boost employee morale and productivity. Engaged and motivated teams are more likely to collaborate effectively and achieve high performance.

2. **Long-Term Organizational Success**: Organizations led by sustainable leaders are better equipped to navigate challenges and seize opportunities. Their focus on long-term goals and ethical practices builds resilience and stability, ensuring sustained success.

3. **Positive Social and Environmental Impact**: Sustainable leaders are committed to making a difference beyond their organization. They actively seek to reduce their environmental footprint and contribute to the

well-being of their communities. This commitment to social responsibility enhances the organization's reputation and fosters trust among stakeholders.

**Examples of Sustainable Leadership in Action**

To illustrate the principles of sustainable leadership, consider the following case studies:

1. **Patagonia:** Leading with Environmental Stewardship - Patagonia, the outdoor clothing and gear company, exemplifies sustainable leadership through its commitment to environmental sustainability. Founder Yvon Chouinard has integrated environmental responsibility into the company's core mission. Patagonia donates a significant portion of its profits to environmental causes, uses sustainable materials, and encourages customers to buy fewer products by promoting repair and reuse. This long-term vision has built a loyal customer base and established Patagonia as a leader in corporate social responsibility.

2. **Unilever**: Balancing Profit and Purpose - Under the leadership of former CEO Paul Polman, Unilever adopted a sustainable business model that balances profit with social and environmental goals. The company's Sustainable Living Plan aims to decouple growth from environmental impact while increasing positive social impact. By focusing on sustainability, Unilever has improved its brand image, reduced costs, and driven innovation. This holistic approach has resulted in long-term growth and a positive societal impact.

**Comparative Analysis: Traditional vs. Sustainable Leadership**

To understand the advantages of sustainable leadership, it is helpful to compare it with traditional leadership models.

Traditional leaders often prioritize immediate results and short-term gains. This can lead to decisions that boost short-term performance but compromise long-term sustainability. In contrast, sustainable leaders emphasize long-term success, ensuring that their actions today support future growth and stability.

### Authority vs. Influence

Traditional leadership relies heavily on authority and control. Leaders make decisions and expect compliance from their team members. Sustainable leadership, however, is based on influence and collaboration. Sustainable leaders inspire and empower others, fostering a sense of ownership and engagement.

### Profit-Driven vs. Purpose-Driven

Traditional leaders typically focus on maximizing profits. While financial performance is important, sustainable leaders balance profit with purpose. They consider the broader impact of their actions on society and the environment, striving to create value for all stakeholders.

### Implementing Sustainable Leadership Practices

To become a sustainable leader, consider the following practices:

1. **Develop a Clear Vision:**
Articulate a long-term vision that aligns with your values and inspires others. Communicate this vision consistently and ensure that it guides your decision-making processes.

2. **Prioritize Ethical Behavior**:
Commit to ethical behavior in all aspects of your leadership. Make decisions based on integrity and fairness, and hold yourself and others accountable to high ethical standards.

3. **Foster a Culture of Learning**:

Encourage continuous learning and development within your organization. Provide opportunities for professional growth and create an environment where mistakes are seen as learning opportunities.

**4. Engage and Empower Your Team**:
Empower your team members by delegating responsibility and encouraging autonomy. Foster open communication and collaboration, and recognize and reward contributions.

**5. Focus on Long-Term Impact**:
Make decisions that support long-term sustainability. Consider the environmental, social, and economic impact of your actions, and strive to create lasting value.

Sustainable leadership is essential for navigating the complexities of today's world. By prioritizing ethical behavior, visionary thinking, and long-term success, sustainable leaders create positive and lasting impact. As you embark on your journey to become a sustainable leader, remember that true leadership extends beyond authority. It is about inspiring others, fostering innovation, and building a legacy of enduring success.

In the following chapters, we will explore the specific skills and strategies needed to develop and implement sustainable leadership practices. From cultivating a leadership mindset to empowering your team and navigating ethical dilemmas, this book will provide you with the tools and insights necessary to lead effectively and sustainably.

Chapter 2

**Cultivating a Leadership Mindset:preface to Leadership Mindset**

Effective leadership begins with mindset — the underpinning beliefs, stations, and perspectives that shape how leaders suppose and act. In this chapter, we explore the significance of cultivating a growth mindset, developing emotional intelligence, and fostering tone- mindfulness as foundational rudiments of sustainable leadership. The Growth Mindset The growth mindset, vulgarized by psychologist Carol Dweck, emphasizes the belief that capacities and intelligence can be developed through fidelity and hard work. Leaders with a growth mindset see challenges as openings for growth, grasp failure as a literacy experience, and persist in the face of lapses.

**Practical way to Develop a Growth Mindset**

1. Embrace Challenges in, impulses, and responses, especially in stressful or grueling situations.

2. Learn from Failure: Shift your perspective on failure from something to be feared to something to be embraced. Analyze failures to extract lessons and insights for future success.

3. provocation The drive to achieve pretensions, persist in the face of lapses, and maintain a positive outlook.

4. Empathy The capability to understand and partake the passions and perspectives of others, fostering connection and collaboration.

5. Social Chops Proficiency in structure and maintaining connections, communicating effectively, and resolving conflicts.

**Ways for Enhancing Emotional Intelligence**

1. Practice tone- Reflection Set away time for soul-searching and reflection to increase tone- mindfulness and identify areas for enhancement.

2. Develop Stress operation ways Learn and practice stress reduction ways similar as awareness, deep breathing, and time operation to enhance tone- regulation.

3. Cultivate Empathy laboriously hear to others, put yourself in their shoes, and validate their feelings and gests to strengthen empathy.

4. Enhance Communication Chops Hone your verbal and verbal communication chops, including active listening, fierceness, and clarity in expression.

**Practical Exercises**

1. Journaling Keep a journal to record your studies, feelings, and reflections on leadership gests . Review your entries periodically to identify patterns and areas for growth.

2. part- Playing Engage in part- playing exercises to exercise emotional intelligence chops similar as active listening, empathy, and conflict resolution in simulated scripts.

3. Feedback supplication Seek feedback from associates, instructors, and platoon members on your leadership style and emotional intelligence. Use their perceptivity to inform your development pretensions and action plans.

Cultivating a leadership mindset is essential for sustainable leadership success. By developing a growth mindset, emotional intelligence, and tone- mindfulness, leaders can enhance their capability to inspire and impact others, navigate challenges with adaptability, and foster a culture of nonstop literacy and growth within their associations.

In the following chapters, we will claw deeper into specific leadership practices and strategies for applying these mindset principles in real-world leadership situations.

Chapter 3

**Vision Beyond Authority: Introduction to Visionary Leadership**

In this chapter, I will will explore the transformative power of visionary leadership. Sustainable leaders understand the importance of crafting a compelling vision that goes beyond traditional authority. They inspire and mobilize others toward a shared purpose, creating alignment and direction for their organizations.

### **Creating a Compelling Vision**

A compelling vision serves as a guiding beacon, inspiring and motivating individuals to work towards a common goal. Sustainable leaders articulate a vision that is aspirational, yet attainable, capturing the hearts and minds of their team members.

**Elements of a Strong Vision Statement**

1. **Clarity**: A clear and concise statement that communicates the organization's purpose, values, and goals.

2. **Inspiration**: An inspiring message that resonates with stakeholders, igniting passion and commitment.

3. **Alignment**: A vision that aligns with the organization's values, mission, and long-term objectives.

4. **Flexibility**: A vision that is adaptable to changing circumstances and evolving needs.

### **Communicating Your Vision**

Effective communication is key to ensuring that the vision resonates with all stakeholders. Sustainable leaders use storytelling, visuals, and interactive forums to convey their vision in a compelling and memorable way.

Techniques For Effective Communication

1. **Storytelling**: Craft narratives that illustrate the impact and significance of the vision, making it relatable and tangible.

2. **Visuals**: Use visual aids such as charts, graphs, and videos to enhance understanding and retention.

3. **Interactive Forums**: Engage stakeholders in dialogue and collaboration, soliciting feedback and fostering ownership of the vision.

**Inspiring and Mobilizing Others**

A sustainable leader's ability to inspire and mobilize others is critical to the success of the vision. By modeling enthusiasm, commitment, and resilience, leaders cultivate a culture of trust, collaboration, and shared purpose.

**Methods for Inspiring and Mobilizing Others**

1. **Lead by Example**: Demonstrate alignment with the vision through your actions, decisions, and behaviors.

2. **Empowerment**: Delegate authority and responsibility, empowering individuals to contribute to the realization of the vision.

3. **Recognition**: Acknowledge and celebrate progress and achievements, reinforcing commitment and motivation.

4. **Alignment**: Ensure that organizational structures, processes, and incentives support the vision, fostering coherence and alignment.

**Real-World Examples**

To illustrate the principles of visionary leadership, consider the following case studies:

1. Tesla: Revolutionizing the Automotive Industry
   - Tesla's CEO, Elon Musk, has a bold vision to accelerate the world's transition to sustainable energy. Through innovative products such as electric vehicles and solar energy solutions, Tesla is disrupting the automotive industry and driving toward a more sustainable future.

2. Microsoft: Empowering Every Person and Every Organization
   - Under the leadership of CEO Satya Nadella, Microsoft has embraced a vision to empower individuals and organizations to achieve more. By focusing on innovation, inclusion, and sustainability, Microsoft is transforming the way people work, learn, and connect.

A compelling vision is the cornerstone of sustainable leadership. By articulating a clear and inspiring vision, communicating it effectively, and mobilizing others toward its realization, leaders can create alignment, engagement, and momentum within their team or will explore strategies for building trust and credibility, empowering and enabling others, and leading through influence to bring the vision to life.

Chapter 4

**Building Trust and Credibility**

Trust is the foundation of effective leadership. In this chapter, I'll explore the significance of erecting trust and credibility as essential factors of sustainable leadership. Leaders who prioritize trust produce a positive work terrain, foster collaboration, and inspire fidelity among platoon members. Foundations of Trust in Leadership Trust is erected on a foundation of translucency, thickness, and trustability. Sustainable leaders demonstrate integrity, authenticity, and responsibility in their words and conduct, earning the trust and respect of their platoon members.

**Principles of Trust- Grounded Leadership**

1. translucency Open and honest communication builds trust by fostering clarity and understanding.

2. thickness trustability and pungency in geste and decision- making support trust over time.

3. Integrity Alignment between values, intentions, and conduct enhances credibility and responsibility.

4. Responsibility Taking power of miscalculations and commitments demonstrates responsibility and integrity. Earning and Maintaining Credibility Credibility is essential for effective leadership.
Sustainable leaders establish credibility by demonstrating moxie, capability, and a track record of success. They inspire confidence and trust through their knowledge, chops, and professionalism.

## Strategies for erecting Credibility

1. nonstop literacy Stay informed about assiduity trends, stylish practices, and arising technologies to maintain moxie and applicability.

2. Professional Development Invest in ongoing training and skill development to enhance capability and credibility.

3. Results exposure Deliver palpable results and issues that demonstrate capability and effectiveness in achieving pretensions.

4. Authenticity Be genuine and authentic in your relations, demonstrating sincerity and trustability.

## Building Trust within Team

Trust is essential for effective cooperation and collaboration. Sustainable leaders produce a culture of trust by fostering open communication, collective respect, and cerebral safety within their team.

### Strategies for Building Trust within brigades

1. Open Communication Encourage translucency and dialogue, creating openings for platoon members to state their opinions and enterprises.

2. Empathy and Respect Demonstrate empathy and respect for different perspectives and gests , fostering a sense of belonging and addition.

3. Conflict Resolution Address conflicts constructively and hypercritically, seeking mutually salutary judgments that save trust and connections.

4. thickness and Fairness Apply rules, programs, and opinions constantly and fairly, erecting trust through indifferent treatment.

**Real- World exemplifications**

To illustrate the principles of trust- grounded leadership, consider the following case studies:

1. Zappos Cultivating a Culture of Trust - Zappos, the online shoe and apparel retailer, is famed for its client- centric culture and hand commission. CEO Tony Hsieh prioritized trust and translucency, creating a plant where workers feel valued, admired, and trusted to make opinions.

2. Warby Parker Building Credibility through Social Responsibility - Warby Parker, the eyewear retailer, has erected credibility through its commitment to social responsibility and ethical business practices. By transparently communicating its charge, values, and impact, Warby Parker has earned the trust and fidelity of guests and workers likewise.

Trust and credibility are necessary rates of sustainable leadership. By prioritizing translucency, integrity, and responsibility, leaders can make trust within their brigades and inspire confidence in their stakeholders. In the following chapters, I'll explore strategies for empowering and enabling others, leading through influence, and navigating ethical dilemmas to foster sustainable success.

Chapter 5

**Empowering and Enabling Others**

Empowering and enabling others is a hallmark of sustainable leadership. In this chapter, I will explore the importance of empowering team members, fostering autonomy, and creating an environment where individuals can unleash their full potential.

**The Power of Empowerment**

Empowerment involves delegating authority, granting autonomy, and providing support and resources to enable individuals to take ownership of their work and make meaningful contributions to the organization. Sustainable leaders recognize the value of empowering others and creating a culture of trust, accountability, and innovation.

**Benefits of Empowering Others**

1. **Increased Motivation and Engagement**: Empowered individuals feel a sense of ownership and responsibility, leading to higher levels of motivation and engagement.

2. **Enhanced Creativity and Innovation**: Autonomy and freedom to experiment foster creativity and innovation, driving continuous improvement and adaptation.

3. **Improved Decision-Making**: Empowered individuals are better positioned to make informed decisions and solve problems independently, leading to more agile and effective decision-making processes.

4. **Greater Organizational Agility:** Empowerment decentralizes decision-making and enables faster responses to changing conditions, enhancing organizational agility and resilience.

### Creating a Culture of Empowerment

Building a culture of empowerment requires a shift in leadership mindset and organizational practices. Sustainable leaders establish clear expectations, provide resources and support, and celebrate autonomy and initiative.

### Strategies for Creating a Culture of Empowerment

1. **Clarify Roles and Expectations**: Clearly define roles, responsibilities, and performance expectations to provide a framework for autonomy and accountability.

2. **Provide Resources and Support**: Equip individuals with the tools, training, and resources they need to succeed, and offer guidance and mentorship as needed.

3. **Encourage Risk-Taking**: Foster a culture that embraces experimentation and learning from failure, encouraging individuals to take calculated risks and explore new ideas.

4. **Recognize and Reward Initiative**: Acknowledge and celebrate individuals who demonstrate initiative, innovation, and results, reinforcing a culture of empowerment and excellence.

### Enabling Growth and Development

Empowerment goes hand in hand with growth and development. Sustainable leaders invest in the growth and development of their team members, providing opportunities for learning, skill development, and career advancement.

### Strategies for Enabling Growth and Development:

1. **Offer Learning Opportunities:** Provide access to training programs, workshops, and educational resources to enhance skills and knowledge.

2. **Assign Challenging Projects:** Assign challenging projects and stretch assignments that offer opportunities for growth and development.

3. **Encourage Mentorship and Coaching:** Facilitate mentorship and coaching relationships to provide guidance, feedback, and support for professional development.

4. **Promote Career Mobility**: Encourage career exploration and mobility within the organization, allowing individuals to pursue opportunities aligned with their interests and aspirations.

### Real-World Examples

To illustrate the principles of empowerment in leadership, consider the following case studies:

1. Google: Empowering Innovation Through 20% Time
- Google's famous "20% time" policy allows employees to spend a portion of their work hours on personal projects of their choosing. This initiative has led to the development of innovative products and features, demonstrating the power of autonomy and empowerment in driving creativity and innovation.

2. Gore: A Culture of Empowerment and Collaboration
- W.L. Gore & Associates, the maker of Gore-Tex fabrics, has built a culture of empowerment and collaboration based on its "lattice" organizational structure. Employees are encouraged to take on leadership roles and make decisions autonomously, leading to a highly innovative and agile organization.

Empowering and enabling others is essential for sustainable leadership. By creating a culture of trust, autonomy, and growth, leaders can unleash the full potential of their team members, driving innovation, engagement, and organizational success. In the following chapters, we will explore strategies for leading through influence, navigating ethical dilemmas, and it.

Chapter 6

## Leading Through Influence

Sustainable leadership often relies more on influence than authority. In this chapter, I will explore the art of leading through influence, examining how leaders can inspire, persuade, and motivate others without relying solely on positional power.

### Understanding Influence

Influence is the capacity to affect the character, development, or behavior of someone or something. Unlike authority, which is rooted in formal power, influence stems from interpersonal skills, relationships, and the ability to inspire and persuade.

### Key Components of Influence

1. **Credibility**: Being trustworthy and competent builds the foundation for influence.

2. **Relationship** Building: Establishing strong, genuine relationships enhances the ability to influence others.

3. **Communication Skills**: Effective communication is crucial for conveying ideas and persuading others.

4. **Emotional Intelligence**: Understanding and managing emotions helps in navigating social complexities and influencing others effectively.

### Strategies for Leading Through Influence

1. **Building Credibility and Trust:**

Credibility is earned through consistent actions, expertise, and integrity. Leaders who demonstrate reliability and competence are more likely to be trusted and respected.

i - **Demonstrate Expertise**: Share your knowledge and skills to establish yourself as a subject matter expert.

ii - **Be Consistent:** Align your actions with your words and values, ensuring that others can rely on you.

ii - **Show Integrity:** Act with honesty and fairness, even in challenging situations.

2. **Cultivating Relationships**:

Building strong relationships is essential for influence. Leaders who invest in relationships create a network of allies and supporters.

i - **Show Genuine Interest**: Take time to understand the needs, aspirations, and concerns of others.

ii - **Be Empathetic**: Demonstrate empathy by actively listening and validating others' perspectives.

iii - **Offer Support:** Provide assistance and resources to help others succeed, fostering goodwill and reciprocity.

3. **Mastering Communication:**

Effective communication is a powerful tool for influence. Leaders who can articulate their vision and ideas clearly and persuasively are more likely to inspire and mobilize others.

i - **Tailor Your Message**: Adapt your communication style to resonate with your audience's values and interests.

ii - **Use Stories and Examples**: Share compelling stories and examples to illustrate your points and make your message memorable.

ii - **Engage in Active Listening**: Listen attentively to feedback and concerns, demonstrating respect and openness.

4. **Leveraging Emotional Intelligence**

Emotional intelligence enables leaders to navigate interpersonal dynamics and influence others effectively.

i - **Self-Awareness**: Recognize your own emotions and how they affect your interactions.

ii - **Self-Regulation**: Manage your emotions and reactions, especially in stressful situations.

ii - **Social Awareness**: Understand the emotions and dynamics of those around you.

iv - **Relationship Management**: Use emotional intelligence to build and maintain strong relationships.

### Influencing Upward and Laterally

Effective leaders influence not only their direct reports but also their peers and superiors. This requires a nuanced approach and an understanding of organizational dynamics.

### Strategies for Influencing Upward

1. **Understand Their Priorities**: Align your proposals and ideas with the goals and priorities of your superiors.

2. **Provide Solutions:** Offer well-thought-out solutions rather than just presenting problems.

3. **Build Alliances:** Foster relationships with key influencers and decision-makers to gain support for your initiatives.

### Strategies for Influencing Laterally

1. **Collaborate and Share Credit:** Work collaboratively with peers and share credit for successes, fostering a culture of teamwork.

2. **Find Common Ground:** Identify shared goals and interests to build rapport and cooperation.

3. **Communicate Effectively**: Use clear, respectful, and persuasive communication to gain buy-in from colleagues.

### Real-World Examples

To illustrate the principles of influence-based leadership, consider the following case studies:

1. Nelson Mandela: Leading Through Influence and Reconciliation
 - Nelson Mandela, South Africa's first black president, exemplified leading through influence. He used his credibility, communication skills, and emotional intelligence to promote reconciliation and unity in a deeply divided nation.

2. Indra Nooyi: Influencing Through Empathy and Vision
As CEO of PepsiCo, Indra Nooyi influenced stakeholders by articulating a clear vision for the company's future and demonstrating empathy and

understanding toward employees and customers, fostering a strong and supportive corporate culture.

Leading through influence is a critical skill for sustainable leadership. By building credibility, cultivating relationships, mastering communication, and leveraging emotional intelligence, leaders can inspire and mobilize others toward shared goals. In the following chapters, I will explore strategies for navigating ethical dilemmas, fostering resilience, and sustaining long-term success.

Chapter 7

**Navigating Ethical Dilemmas: Introduction to Ethical Leadership**

Ethical leadership is integral to sustainable success. In this chapter, I examine how leaders can navigate ethical dilemmas, maintain integrity, and foster a culture of ethical behavior within their organizations.

**The Importance of Ethical Leadership**

Ethical leadership involves making decisions that are morally sound and aligning actions with core values. Leaders who prioritize ethics build trust, enhance their credibility, and create a positive organizational culture. Ethical leadership is not only about compliance with laws and regulations but also about doing what is right, even when it is difficult.

**Benefits of Ethical Leadership**

1. **Enhanced Trust and Reputation**: Ethical behavior builds trust among stakeholders and enhances the organization's reputation.

2. **Increased Employee Engagement**: Employees are more engaged and motivated when they perceive their leaders and organization as ethical.

3. **Sustainable Success**: Ethical leadership promotes long-term success by fostering loyalty and reducing the risk of legal and reputational issues.

4. **Positive Organizational Culture**: An ethical culture attracts talent, reduces turnover, and creates a supportive and collaborative work environment.

## Identifying Ethical Dilemmas

Ethical dilemmas often involve complex situations where the right course of action is not clear-cut. Leaders must be able to identify and analyze these dilemmas to make informed and ethical decisions.

### Types of Ethical Dilemmas

1. **Conflict of Interest**: Situations where personal interests conflict with professional responsibilities.

2. **Resource Allocation**: Decisions about how to distribute limited resources fairly and equitably.

3. **Confidentiality and Transparency**: Balancing the need for confidentiality with the obligation for transparency and honesty.

4. **Fair Treatment:** Ensuring fair and unbiased treatment of all employees and stakeholders.

### Framework for Ethical Decision-Making

A structured approach to ethical decision-making helps leaders navigate dilemmas effectively. The following framework provides a systematic process for making ethical decisions.

### Steps in Ethical Decision-Making

1. Identify the Ethical Issues: Clearly define the ethical dilemma and identify the stakeholders involved.

2. **Gather Relevant Information**: Collect all relevant facts and consider the perspectives of all stakeholders.

3. **Evaluate Alternatives:** Consider the potential outcomes and ethical implications of different courses of action.

4. **Make a Decision:** Choose the action that aligns with ethical principles and values.

5. **Implement the Decision**: Act on the decision and communicate it transparently to those affected.

6. **Reflect and Learn**: Reflect on the decision-making process and the outcomes to learn and improve for future dilemmas.

### Building an Ethical Culture

Creating a culture of ethics requires intentional efforts and consistent actions from leaders. Sustainable leaders embed ethical principles into the organization's values, policies, and practices.

### Methods for Building an Ethical Culture

1. **Set the Tone at the Top:** Leaders must model ethical behavior and demonstrate a commitment to ethics in their actions and decisions.

2. **Develop Clear Policies**: Establish clear ethical guidelines and policies that outline expected behaviors and decision-making processes.

3. **Provide Ethics Training**: Offer regular training and education on ethical principles, dilemmas, and decision-making frameworks.

4. **Encourage Open Communication**: Foster an environment where employees feel safe to speak up about ethical concerns and dilemmas.

5. Establish Accountability Mechanisms: Implement systems for monitoring and enforcing ethical behavior, including reporting mechanisms and disciplinary actions.

**Real-World Examples**

To illustrate the principles of ethical leadership, consider the following case studies:

1. Johnson & Johnson: The Tylenol Crisis
   - In 1982, Johnson & Johnson faced a major ethical dilemma when cyanide-laced Tylenol capsules resulted in multiple deaths. The company's decision to prioritize consumer safety by recalling all Tylenol products and implementing tamper-resistant packaging is a classic example of ethical leadership.

2. Patagonia: Commitment to Environmental Ethics- Patagonia, the outdoor apparel company, is known for its commitment to environmental sustainability. The company's leadership consistently makes ethical decisions that prioritize environmental responsibility, such as using sustainable materials and donating a portion of profits to environmental causes.

Navigating ethical dilemmas is a critical aspect of sustainable leadership. By adopting a structured approach to ethical decision-making, building an ethical culture, and modeling integrity, leaders can ensure that their organizations uphold ethical standards and values. In the following chapters, I will explore strategies for fostering resilience, leading through change, and sustaining long-term success.

Chapter 8

**Fostering Adaptability in Leadership**

Adaptability is the capacity to recover snappily from difficulties and acclimatize to adversity. In this chapter, we claw into the significance of adaptability in leadership, exploring strategies for developing particular adaptability and fostering adaptability within brigades and associations.
The significance of Resilience flexible leaders are better equipped to navigate challenges, maintain stability, and drive sustained success. They can manage stress, acclimatize to change, and inspire confidence in their brigades during turbulent times. structure adaptability helps leaders and their associations thrive amid query and dislocation.

**Benefits of flexible Leadership**

1. Enhanced Rigidity flexible leaders can pivot and acclimatize to changing circumstances, icing organizational dexterity.

2. Advanced Stress operation flexible leaders manage stress effectively, maintaining their well- being and performance.

3. Greater Persistence flexible leaders persist through lapses, maintaining focus on long- term pretensions.

4. Positive part Modeling flexible leaders serve as part models, inspiring their brigades to develop their adaptability.

**Developing particular Adaptability**

particular adaptability begins with tone- mindfulness and tone- care. Leaders must fete their stressors, understand their managing mechanisms, and prioritize their physical and internal well- being.

**Strategies for Building Personal Resilience**

1. **tone-mindfulness and Reflection:**
 i- Identify Stressors Fete the situations, tasks, and relations that spark stress. Keep a journal to track stressors and your responses.

ii- Reflect on gests Regularly reflect on grueling gests and how you managed them. Identify what worked well and areas for enhancement.

2. **Stress operation ways:**
i- awareness and Contemplation Practice awareness and contemplation to stay present and manage stress. ways like deep breathing and progressive muscle relaxation can also help.

ii-Physical exertion Engage in regular physical exertion to reduce stress and ameliorate overall well- being. Exercise can be a important stress reliever and mood supporter.

iii-Acceptable Rest Prioritize sleep and relaxation. insure you get enough rest to recharge and recover.

3. **Emotional Intelligence**:
 i -Tone-Regulation Develop the capability to manage your feelings, especially under pressure. Practice ways like breaking before replying andre-framing negative studies.

ii- Empathy Cultivate empathy to more understand and connect with others, enhancing your capability to support and lead your platoon effectively.

4. **Positive Mindset and sanguinity**:
i - Cultivate sanguinity Focus on positive aspects and implicit results rather than dwelling on problems. Maintain a hopeful outlook indeed in grueling times.

ii - Gratitude Practice Regularly exercise gratefulness to shift focus to the positive aspects of life and leadership. Keeping a gratefulness journal can be salutary. Fostering Team Resilience flexible brigades can handle adversity, support each other, and maintain performance under pressure. Leaders play a pivotal part in structure and sustaining platoon adaptability.

**Strategies for Building Team Resilience**

1. **Promote Psychological Safety**:
i- Encourage Open Communication produce an terrain where platoon members feel safe to express enterprises, share ideas, and admit miscalculations without fear of retaliation.

ii- Foster Inclusivity insure all platoon members feel valued and included. Celebrate different perspectives and benefactions.

2. **figure Strong connections:**
i -platoon-structure Conditioning grease conditioning that make trust and fellowship among platoon members. These conditioning can range from platoon retreats to regular informal gatherings.

ii -probative Culture Encourage platoon members to support each other, feting and addressing signs of stress or collapse among peers.

3. **Encourage Inflexibility and Rigidity:**
i -Cross-Training Promotecross-training and skill development to enhance platoon versatility and rigidity. This prepares platoon members to take on different places as demanded.

ii -nimble Practices apply nimble practices that allow the platoon to respond snappily to changes and unanticipated challenges. Encourage iterative planning and nonstop enhancement.

**4. Fete and Award Adaptability:**
I - Celebrate Successes
Acknowledge and celebrate both small and significant achievements, buttressing a positive and flexible mindset.

ii - give Formative Feedback Offer formative feedback that focuses on growth and literacy. Use lapses as openings for development and enhancement.

### Organizational Resilience

Organizational resilience involves creating systems and processes that enable the organization to withstand shocks and recover from disruptions. It requires a strategic approach to risk management, innovation, and continuous improvement.

**Strategies for Building Organizational Resilience**

**1. Risk Management and Contingency Planning**

I - Identify Risks: Conduct thorough risk assessments to identify potential threats to the organization.

ii - Develop Contingency Plans: Create detailed contingency plans for various scenarios. Ensure all employees are aware of these plans and know their roles in executing them.

**2. Innovation and Continuous Improvement**

I - Foster a Culture of Innovation: Encourage creativity and experimentation within the organization. Support initiatives that seek to improve processes, products, and services.

ii - Continuous Learning: Promote a culture of continuous learning and development. Provide opportunities for employees to upskill and stay abreast of industry trends and best practices.

3. **Strong Leadership and Governance**

- Transparent Leadership: Ensure leaders at all levels are transparent, communicative, and supportive. Transparent leadership builds trust and resilience within the organization.

- Effective Governance: Implement effective governance structures that support decision-making, accountability, and resilience.

### Real-World Examples

To illustrate the principles of resilient leadership, consider the following case studies:

1. Starbucks: Resilience in the Face of Crisis
During the 2008 financial crisis, Starbucks faced significant challenges. CEO Howard Schultz returned to lead the company, focusing on resilience by closing underperforming stores, revamping the menu, and investing in employee training. This strategy helped Starbucks recover and thrive.

2. Toyota: Learning from Failure
In 2010, Toyota faced a massive recall crisis due to safety issues. The company's response, focused on transparency, accountability, and continuous improvement, demonstrated resilience. Toyota overhauled its quality control processes and regained consumer trust.

Furthermore, fostering resilience is essential for sustainable leadership. By developing personal resilience, building resilient teams, and creating resilient organizations, leaders can navigate adversity, maintain stability, and achieve long-term success. In the following chapters, we will explore strategies for leading through change, fostering innovation, and sustaining long-term success.

Chapter 9

**Leading Through Change**

Change is a constant in moment's dynamic business terrain. Effective leaders must navigate their associations through ages of metamorphosis, icing they remain nimble and competitive.

This chapter explores strategies for leading through change, emphasizing the significance of vision, communication, and rigidity. The Nature of Organizational Change Organizational change can take numerous forms, from minor adaptations in processes to significant shifts in strategy, structure, or culture. Change can be driven by internal factors similar as leadership transitions or external factors similar as request trends, technological advancements, and profitable shifts. Anyhow of its source, managing change effectively is pivotal for sustainable leadership.

**Types of Organizational Change**

1. Strategic Change Changes in the association's overall direction or pretensions.

2. Structural Change variations to the association's scale, places, or reporting lines.

3. Process Change Advancements or differences in workflows, procedures, or systems.

4. Cultural Change Shifts in organizational values, actions, or morals. The part of Vision in Leading Change A clear and compelling vision is essential for guiding associations through change.

Leaders must articulate a vision that resonates with their platoon, furnishing a sense of direction and purpose.

## Casting a Vision for Change

1. Define the End thing easily articulate what the association aims to achieve through the change process.

2. Align with Core Values insure the vision aligns with the association's core values and long- term charge.

3. Inspire and Motivate produce a vision that inspires and motivates workers, fostering a sense of participated purpose and commitment.

## Communicating the Vision

1. harmonious Messaging Communicate the vision constantly across all situations of the association.

2. Engage Stakeholders Involve crucial stakeholders in the communication process, icing they understand and support the vision.

3. use Multiple Channels Use colorful communication channels, including meetings, emails, newsletters, and social media, to reach all workers.

Managing the Change Process Effective change operation involves planning, enforcing, and covering the change process. Leaders must be visionary in addressing challenges and icing smooth transitions.

### Steps in the Change operation Process

1. **Assess the Need for Change**
i - Conduct a SWOT Analysis. estimate the association's strengths, sins, openings, and pitfalls to identify the need for change.

ii - Gather Feedback: Collect input from workers, guests, and other stakeholders to understand their perspectives and enterprises.

2. **Develop a Change Plan**

i - Set Clear objects: Define specific, measurable, attainable, applicable, and time-bound( SMART) objects for the change action.

ii - Allocate coffers: Identify and allocate the necessary coffers, including budget, labor force, and technology, to support the change.

iii - produce a Timeline: Develop a realistic timeline for enforcing the change, including crucial mileposts and deadlines.

3. **Apply the Change** - Communicate Beforehand and frequently Keep workers informed throughout the perpetration process, addressing any questions or enterprises.

i - Give Training and Support: Offer training and support to help workers acclimatize to new processes, systems, or places.

ii - Examiner Progress: Track progress against the change plan, making adaptations as demanded to stay on track.

4. **Estimate and Sustain the Change**

i-Assess issues estimate the issues of the change action against the defined objects. Use criteria and feedback to gauge success.

ii- Celebrate Successes Fete and celebrate achievements and mileposts to support positive geste
and morale.

iii-nonstop enhancement Encourage a culture of nonstop enhancement, where feedback is used to upgrade and enhance processes and practices.

## Prostrating Resistance To Change

**Resistance to change:** is a natural response. Leaders must anticipate and address resistance proactively to insure successful change perpetration.

### Strategies For Prostrating Resistance

1. **Understand the Root Causes:**
i- Identify enterprises Engage with workers to understand their enterprises and fears about the change.

ii- Address Misconceptions give clear and accurate information to disband myths and misconstructions about the change.

2. **Involve workers in the Change Process:**
i- Solicit Input Involve workers in planning and decision- making processes to increase their sense of power and commitment.
2. **Empower Change Agents**: Identify and empower change champions within the organization to advocate for and support the change.

3. **Provide Support and Resources**

Offer Training: Provide the necessary training and resources to help employees develop the skills and knowledge needed to adapt to the change.

Ensure Access to Resources: Ensure employees have access to the tools and resources they need to implement the change effectively.

### Communicate Transparently

1. Be Honest and Open: Communicate transparently about the reasons for the change, the expected benefits, and the potential challenges.

2. Maintain Regular Updates: Keep employees informed about the progress of the change initiative and any adjustments made along the way.

### Real-World Examples

To illustrate the principles of leading through change, consider the following case studies:

1. IBM: Reinventing a Legacy Company

In the early 1990s, IBM faced a significant crisis as its traditional hardware business declined. Under the leadership of CEO Lou Gerstner, IBM underwent a dramatic transformation, shifting its focus to services and software. Gerstner's clear vision, effective communication, and strategic change management led IBM to regain its competitive edge.

2. Netflix: Embracing Digital Disruption

Netflix transitioned from a DVD rental service to a leading streaming platform. This strategic shift, driven by a clear vision and proactive change management, enabled Netflix to stay ahead of industry disruption and become a dominant player in digital entertainment.

In conclusion, Leading through change is a vital skill for sustainable leadership. By crafting a compelling vision, managing the change process effectively, and overcoming resistance, leaders can guide their organizations through periods of transformation successfully. In the final chapter, we will explore strategies for sustaining long-term success, emphasizing the importance of continuous improvement, innovation, and adaptability.

Chapter 10

**Achieving Sustainable, Long- Term Success**

Sustaining long- term success is the ultimate thing for any leader and association. This chapter delves into the strategies and principles that help maintain instigation, drive nonstop enhancement, and insure the continuing success of an association.

**The Pillars of Long- Term Success**

Sustainable success is erected on several crucial pillars.They are:
1. nonstop enhancement, 2.innovation, 3.rigidity, and 4.A strong organizational culture. Leaders must concentrate on these areas to insure their associations remain competitive and flexible over time.

1. **Nonstop Enhancement**

nonstop enhancement involves regularly assessing and enhancing processes, products, and services to drive effectiveness and effectiveness. It requires a mindset of ongoing literacy and development.

**Enforcing nonstop enhancement Models**

i - KaizenOriginating from Japan, Kaizen emphasizes small, incremental advancements in all aspects of the association. Encourage workers at all situations to identify and act on openings for enhancement.

ii - Lean Focuses on maximizing value by minimizing waste. spare principles can be applied to streamline processes, reduce costs, and enhance client value.

iii - Six Sigma: A data-driven approach aimed at reducing blights and variability in processes. Six Sigma uses statistical styles to ameliorate quality and performance.

**Fostering a Culture of enhancement**

i - Empower workers Encourage workers to take power of enhancement enterprise. give them with the tools, training, and authority to make changes.

ii - Encourage Experimentation Promote a culture where trial is valued. Allow workers to test new ideas and approaches without fear of failure.

iii -Regular Feedback utensil systems for regular feedback and reflection. Use feedback circles to identify areas for enhancement and track progress.

## 2. Innovation

Innovation is essential for staying competitive and meeting evolving client requirements. It involves creating new value through new ideas, products, services, or processes.

**Encouraging a Culture of Innovation**

- Support Creative Allowing produce an terrain that encourages creative thinking and problem-working. give spaces and coffers for brainstorming and collaboration.

- price Innovation Fete and award innovative ideas and benefactions. impulses can motivate workers to suppose outside the box and pursue invention.

- Leadership Commitment: Leaders should demonstrate a commitment to invention by investing in R&D, supporting invention enterprise, and fostering a threat-tolerant culture.

### Enforcing Innovation Processes

- Idea Generation Establish formal processes for generating and landing ideas. This could include invention shops, suggestion programs, and collaboration tools.

- Rapid Prototyping: Use rapid-fire prototyping and nimble development methodologies to snappily test and reiterate on new ideas. This allows for faster literacy and adaption.

-Cross-Functional Team Formcross-functional Team to work on invention systems. Different perspectives and moxie can enhance creativity and problem-working.

### 3. Rigidity

Rigidity is the capability to respond effectively to changing circumstances and surroundings. Adaptable associations can navigate misgivings and subsidize on arising openings.

### Developing Adaptive Leadership

i - Inflexibility in Allowing Encourage leaders to be open-inclined and flexible in their thinking. They should be willing to pivot strategies and approaches as demanded.

ii- Responsive Decision- Making Develop systems for quick and responsive decision- timber. This includes empowering frontline workers to make opinions and acclimatize to changes.

iii- Script Planning Use script planning to anticipate implicit unborn changes and develop strategies for different scripts. This prepares the association for colorful contingencies.

### Erecting an Agile Organization

i-Nimble Practices Borrow nimble practices that promote iterative development, collaboration, and nonstop feedback. nimble methodologies, similar as Scrum or Kanban, can enhance rigidity.

ii - Decentralized Decision- Making Empower brigades to make opinions locally, without demanding to stay for top-down directives. This accelerates response times and increases dexterity.

iii-Flexible force Chains Develop flexible force chains that can acclimatize to dislocations. Diversify suppliers, apply threat operation practices, and invest in technology to enhance force chain visibility.

## 4.A Strong Organizational Culture

A strong organizational culture aligns workers with the association's values and charge, driving engagement and performance.

### Defining Core Values and Mission

**Core Values:** Clearly define and communicate the core values that guide the organization's actions and decisions. These values should be reflected in all aspects of the organization.

**Mission:** Ensure the organization's mission is purpose-driven and resonates with employees. A compelling mission can inspire and motivate employees to contribute to the organization's success.

**Embedding Culture in Practices**

1.**Onboarding and Training**: Incorporate the organization's values and culture into onboarding and training programs. New employees should understand and embrace the culture from the start.

2.**Leadership by Example:** Leaders should model the values and behaviors they expect from employees. Their actions set the tone for the organization's culture.

3.**Recognition and Rewards:** Recognize and reward behaviors that align with the organization's values. This reinforces the desired culture and encourages others to follow suit.

**Real-World Examples**

To illustrate the principles of sustaining long-term success, consider the following case studies:

1. Apple Inc.: Innovation and Continuous Improvement

Apple's focus on innovation and continuous improvement has driven its long-term success. The company consistently invests in R&D, leading to groundbreaking products such as the iPhone, iPad, and Apple Watch. Apple's culture of design excellence and customer-centricity reinforces its market leadership.

2. Toyota: Lean Manufacturing and Adaptability

Toyota's commitment to lean manufacturing principles and continuous improvement (Kaizen) has made it a leader in the automotive industry. The company's adaptability and focus on quality have allowed it to navigate market fluctuations and maintain its competitive edge.

Moreover, Sustaining long-term success requires a multifaceted approach that emphasizes continuous improvement, innovation, adaptability, and a strong organizational culture. By focusing on these pillars, leaders can ensure their organizations remain resilient and competitive in an ever-changing environment.

As I conclude this book, remember that sustainable leadership is a journey, not a destination. Continuous learning, adaptability, and a commitment to core values will guide you and your organization toward enduring success.

**Conclusion**

As we conclude this journey through the principles of sustainable leadership, it's essential to reflect on the core tenets that we've explored. Leadership is not merely about holding a position of authority; it's about inspiring, nurturing, and driving continuous growth and success within your team and organization. Sustainable leadership extends beyond traditional paradigms, embracing a holistic approach that prioritizes empathy, resilience, and long-term vision.

Throughout this book, we've delved into the critical aspects that define sustainable leadership. From understanding the importance of self-awareness and emotional intelligence to fostering a culture of trust and collaboration, each chapter has underscored the multifaceted nature of true leadership. We've discussed the significance of adaptability in an ever-changing world, the necessity of transparent communication, and the power of leading by example.

One of the central themes that resonate through these pages is the idea that sustainable leadership is deeply rooted in values and principles. It's about leading with integrity, demonstrating humility, and making decisions that are not only beneficial in the short term but also sustainable for the future. As leaders, our actions and decisions create ripples that extend far beyond our immediate environment, influencing the broader ecosystem in which we operate.

Moreover, we've explored the concept of servant leadership, where the leader's primary goal is to serve others. This approach fosters a supportive environment where team members feel valued and empowered, driving their intrinsic motivation and commitment to the collective vision. It's a reminder that the true measure of a leader lies in the success and growth of their followers.

As you move forward in your leadership journey, remember that the path to sustainable success is not a solitary one. Surround yourself with mentors, seek continuous learning, and remain open to feedback. Leadership is a dynamic and evolving practice, and the willingness to adapt and grow is crucial.

In closing, sustainable leadership is an art and a science, blending strategic thinking with compassionate action. It's about leaving a legacy that transcends your tenure, building an enduring foundation for future generations. Embrace the principles outlined in this book, and let them guide you in creating a positive and lasting impact in your sphere of influence.

Thank you for embarking on this journey. May your leadership inspire and uplift, driving sustainable success in all your endeavors.

A. O Osborne.

www.ingramcontent.com/pod-product-compliance
Lightning Source LLC
Chambersburg PA
CBHW082240220526
45479CB00005B/1287